HEY SIS!

**AS GIRLS,
IT IS IMPORTANT THAT WE STICK TOGETHER!
WE ARE SISTERS!
WE MUST LOVE EACH OTHER!
WE MUST SUPPORT EACH OTHER!
WE MUST PROTECT EACH OTHER!**

-TYIA

Wait! Before you start reading, LOOK!

Things you will need while reading this book:

-crayons
-creativity

Author Note:

Did you know that your friends can be your sisters? As you are reading and drawing, remember that the word sister does not just mean your biological sister. It means every girl in the world! We are all sisters!

**SPECIAL THANKS TO JA'DYN & JONIYAH FOR BEING AMAZING MODELS!
YOU TWO ARE AWESOME!**

ISBN-13: 9798595346184
Copyright © 2020 by tyia adair
published by A Beautiful, Wonderful Me

No part of this book may be used or reproduced in any manner whatsoever without written permission from the author. For more information email: info@abwme.com

I GOT YOU SIS

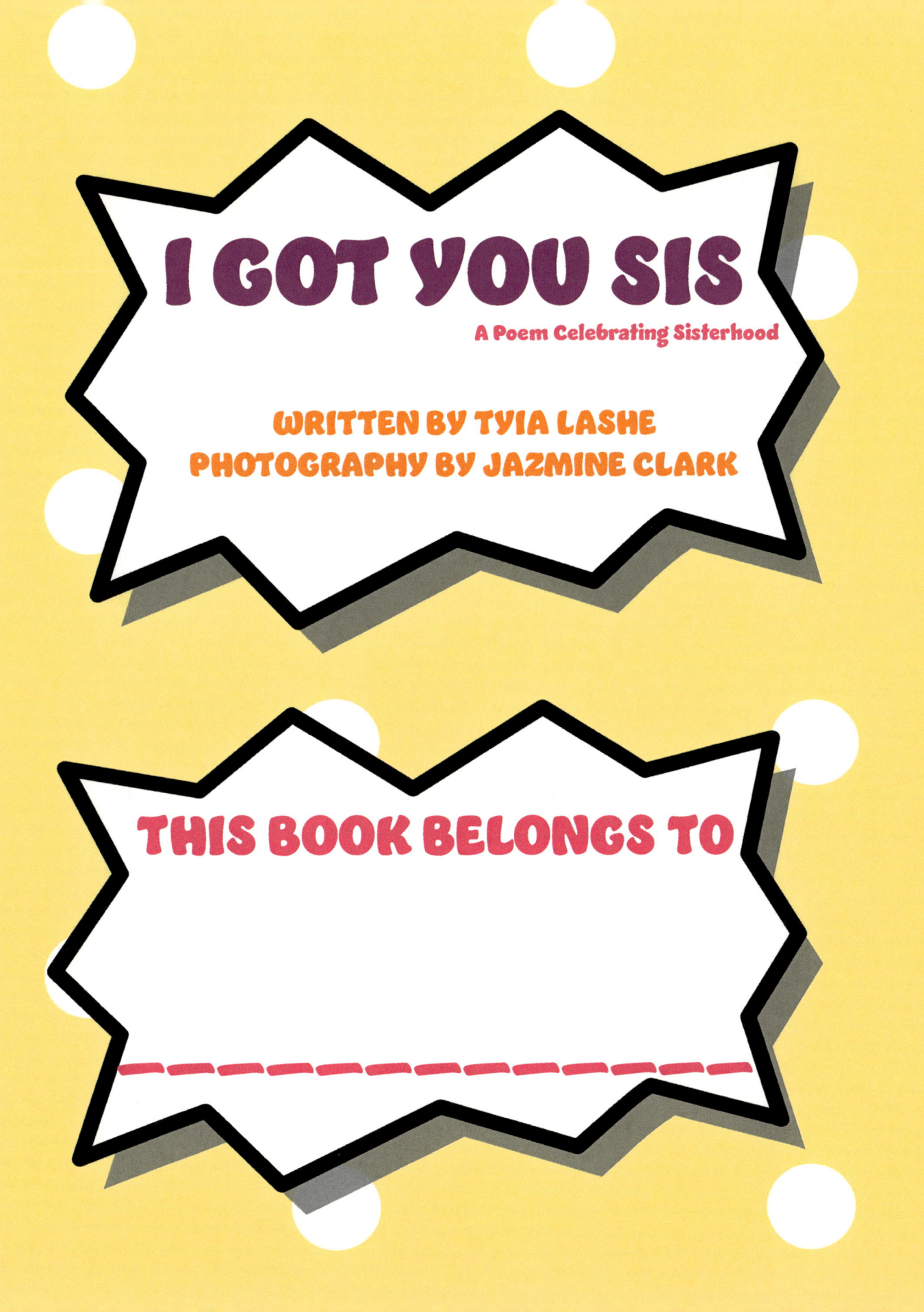

A Poem Celebrating Sisterhood

WRITTEN BY TYIA LASHE
PHOTOGRAPHY BY JAZMINE CLARK

THIS BOOK BELONGS TO

_____

**Girls rock and that's a fact!
There's not a single soul
that can debate that!**

YOU ROCK!

COLOR ME!

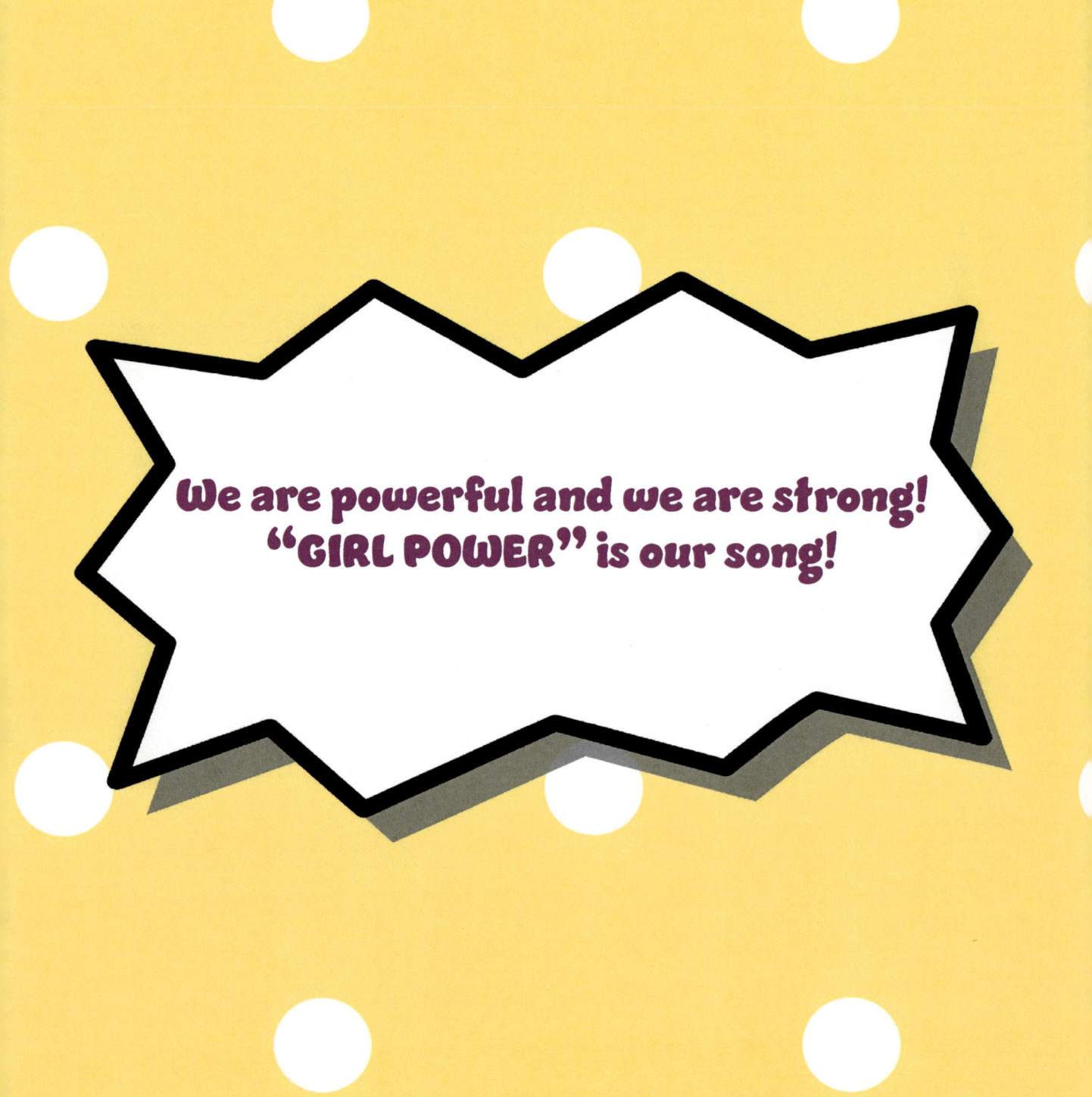

We are powerful and we are strong!
"GIRL POWER" is our song!

GIRL POWER!

COLOR ME!

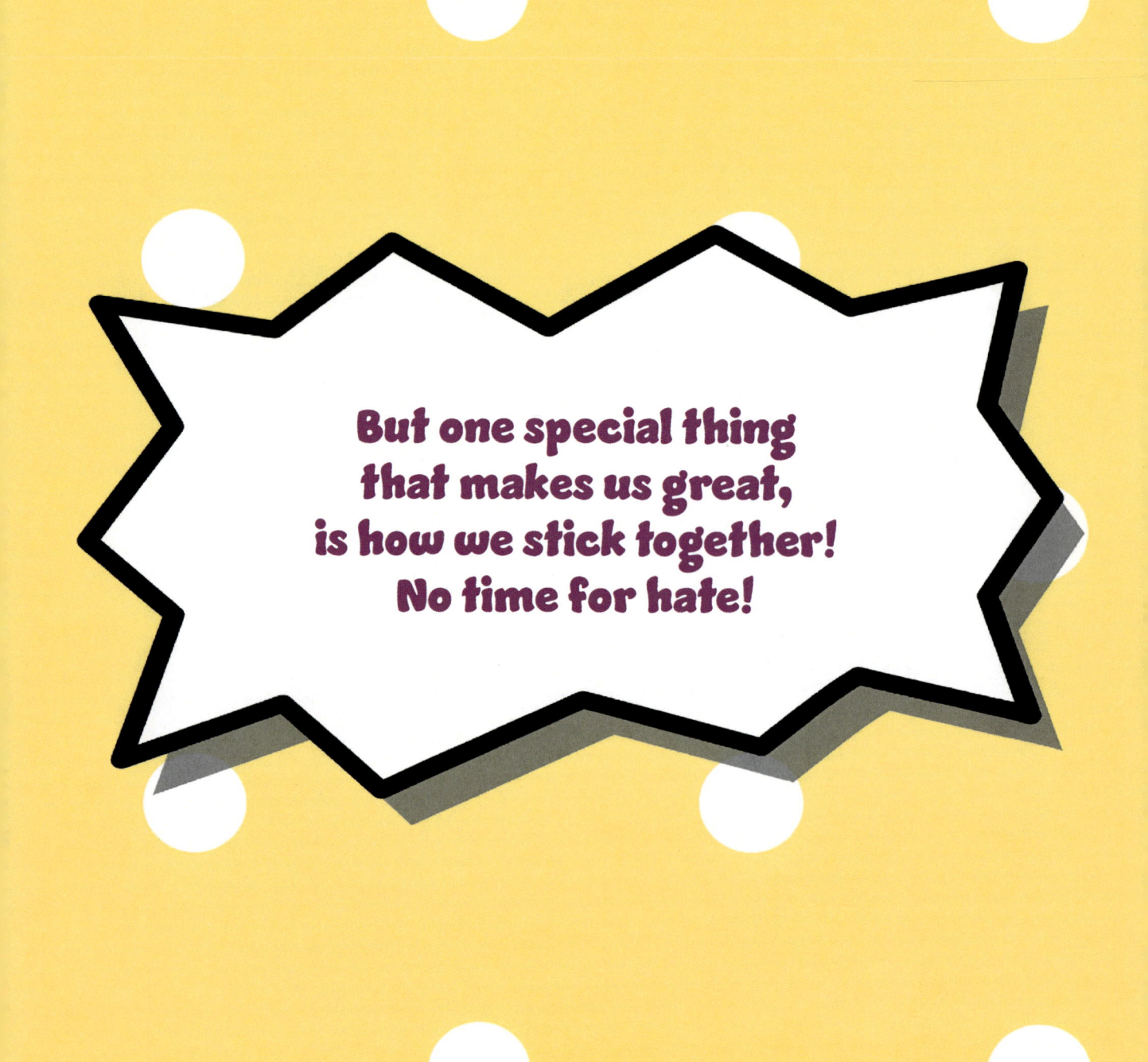

But one special thing
that makes us great,
is how we stick together!
No time for hate!

COLOR ME!

NO HATE!

When I see my sister down,
I help her back up!
I encourage her
to step it up!

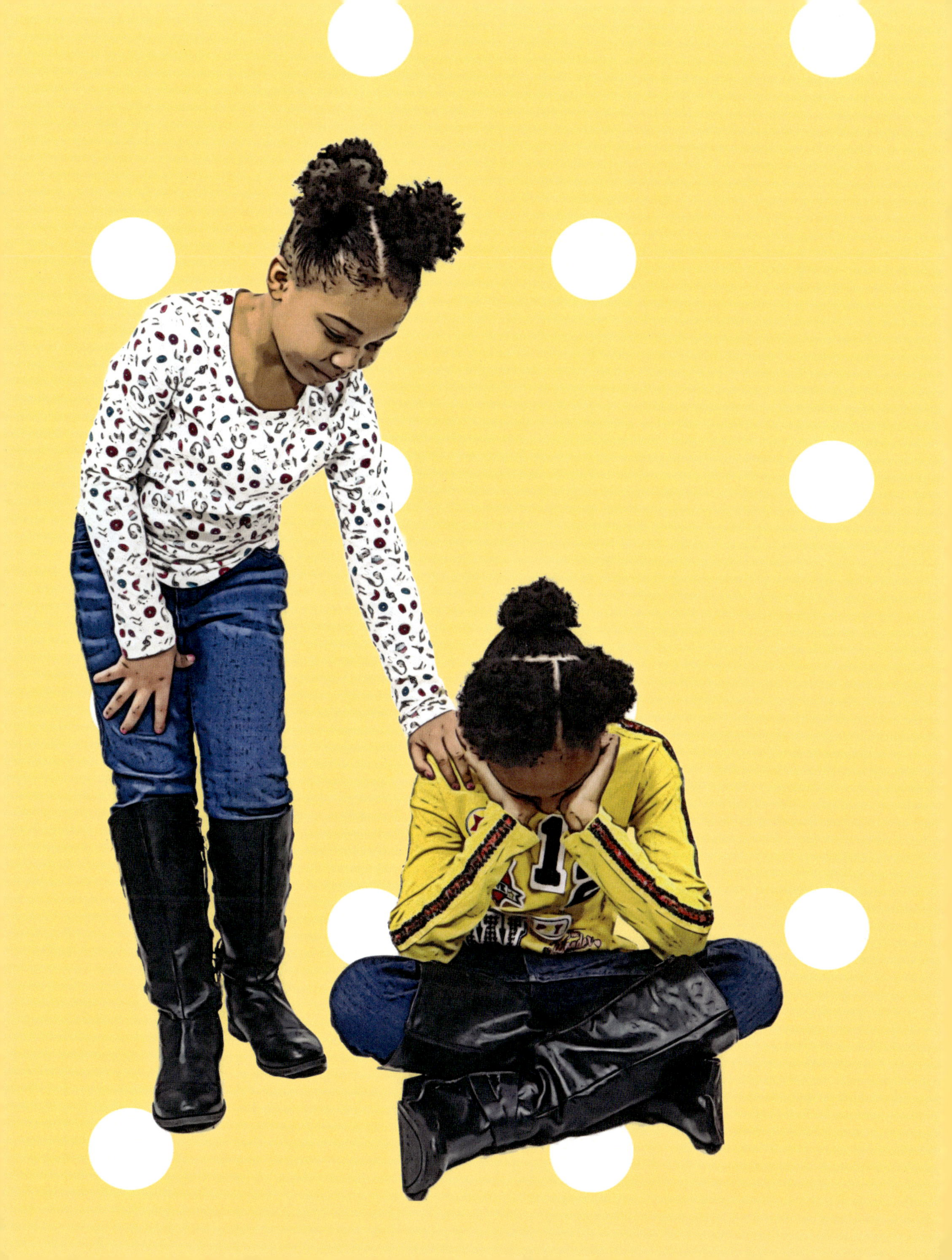

I GOT YOU SIS!

COLOR ME!

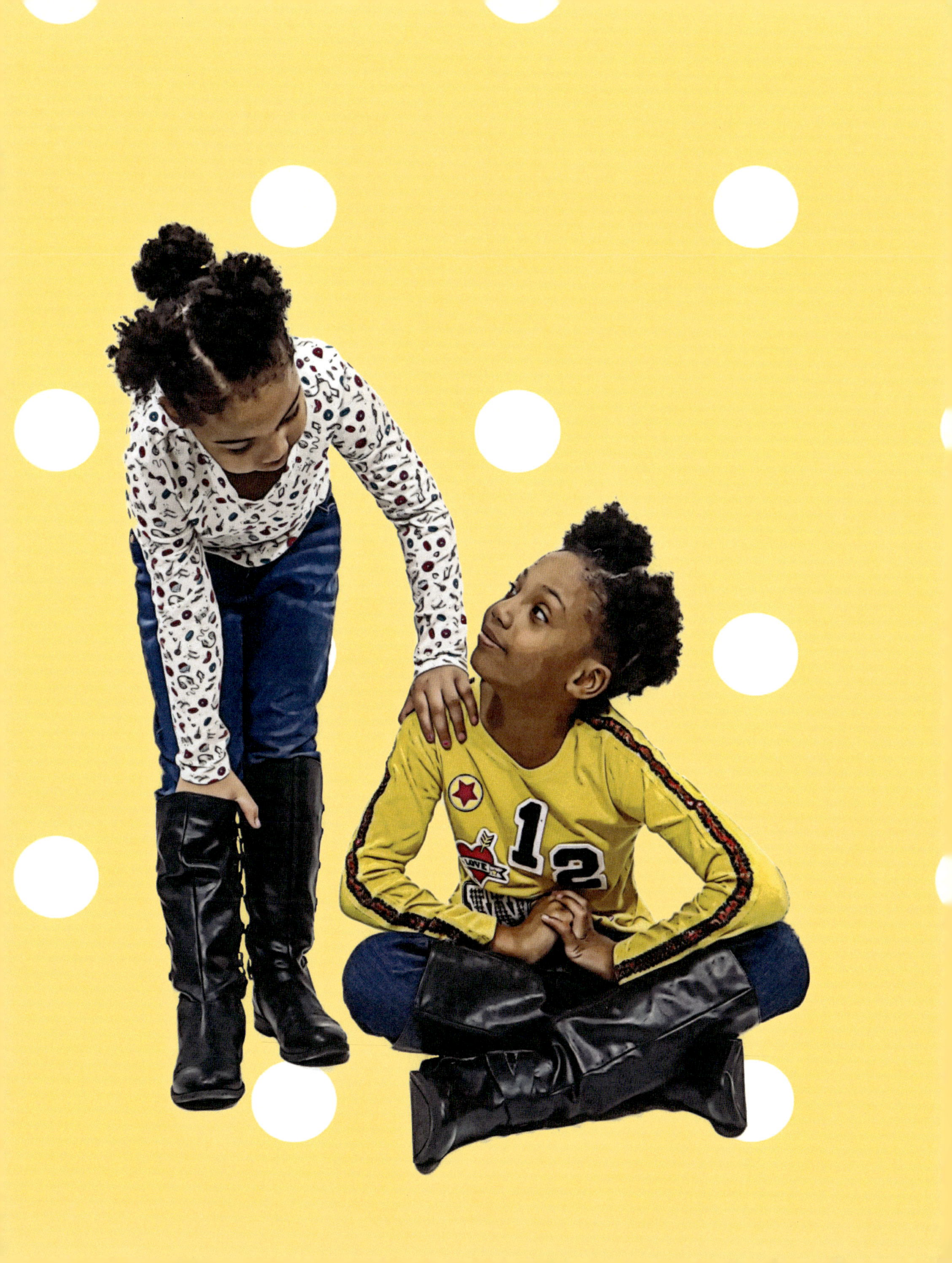
12

When I see my sister win,
I'm the loudest to cheer!
It's only celebrations!
No jealousy here!

CELEBRATIONS ONLY!

Color me!

IT'S ALL LOVE SIS!

COLOR ME!

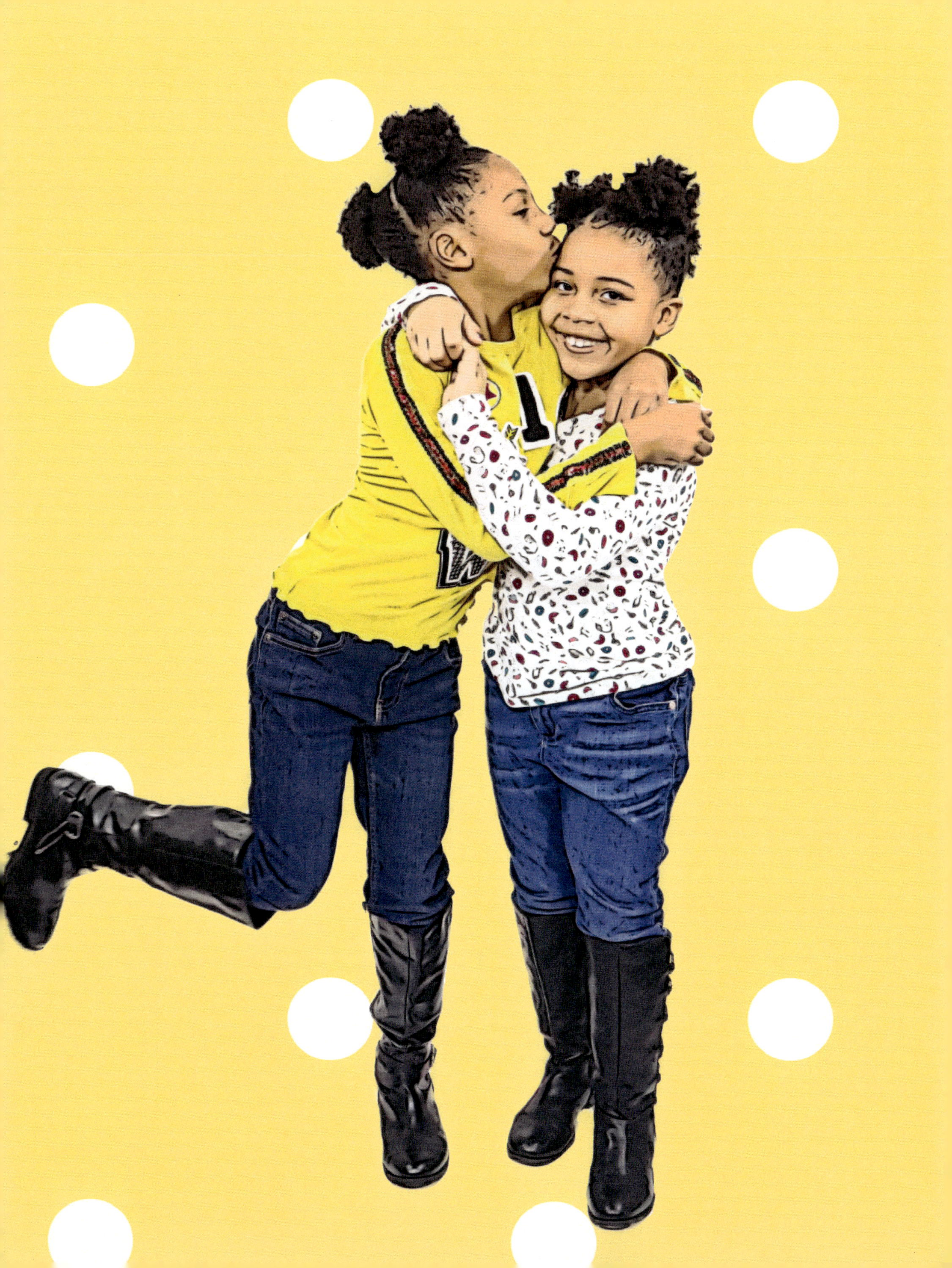

Because when one girl wins, we all win!
When one girl shines, we all shine!

SHINE ON!

Color me!

YOU GO SIS!

COLOR ME!

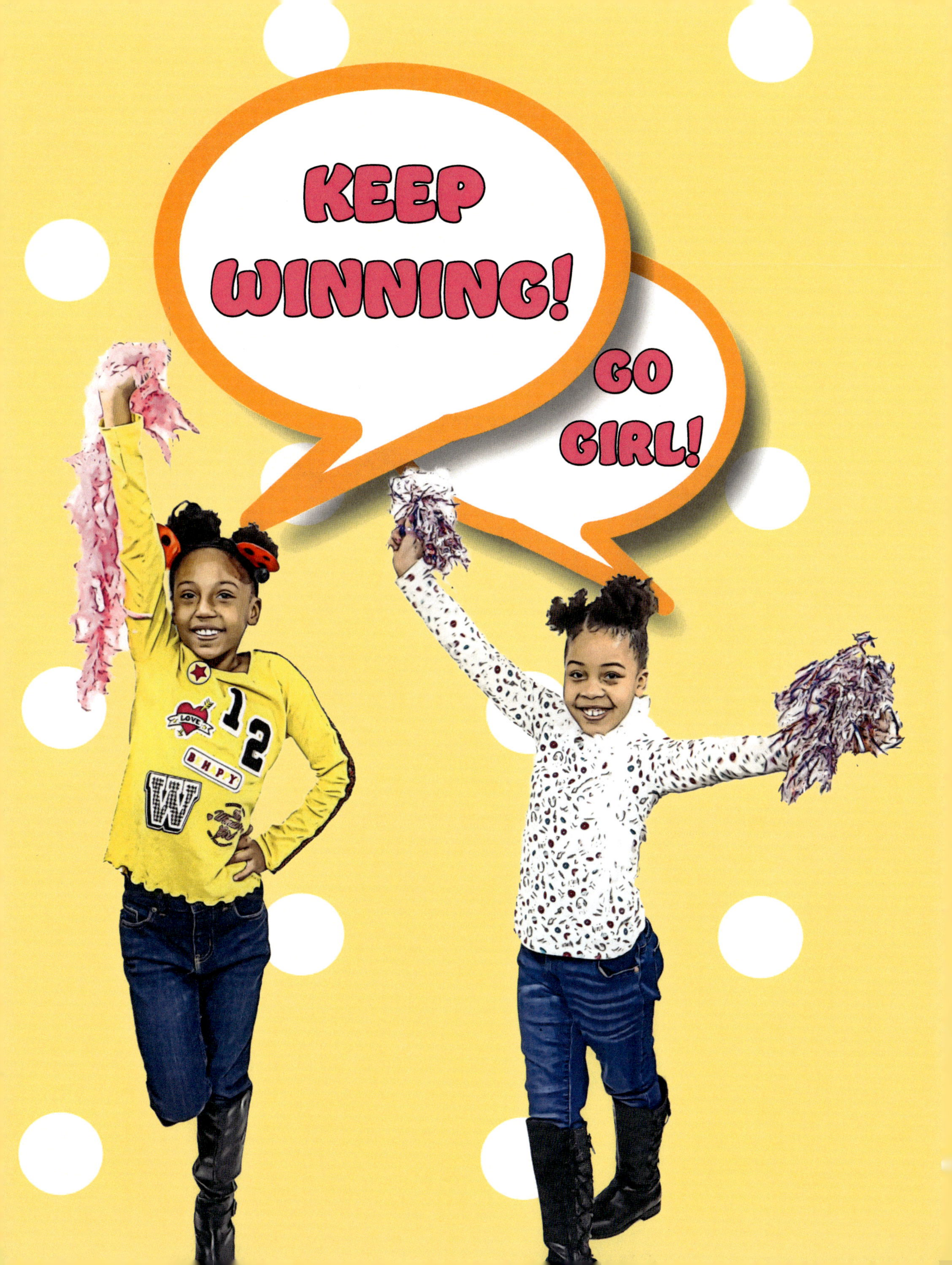
KEEP WINNING!
GO GIRL!

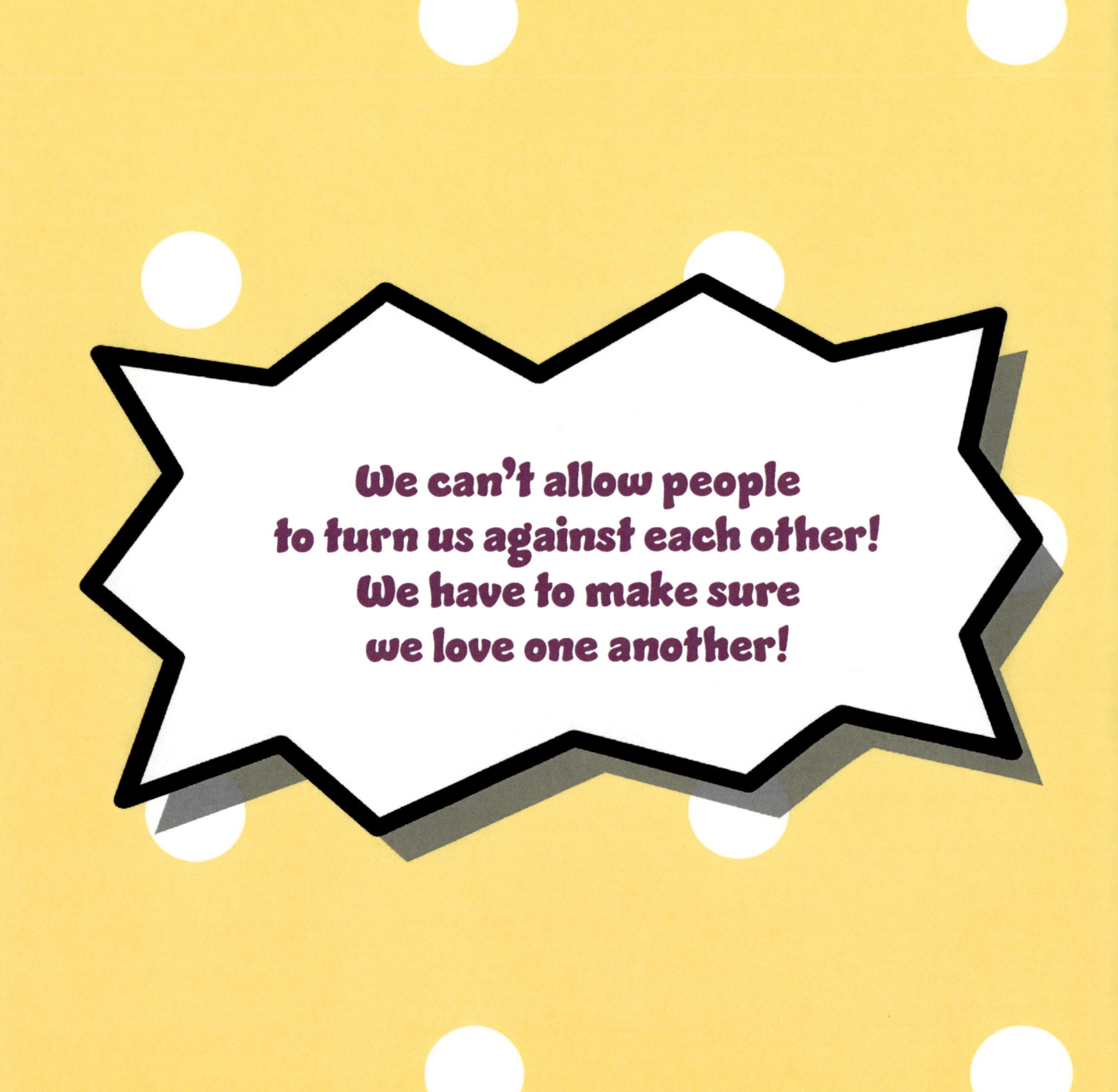

We can't allow people
to turn us against each other!
We have to make sure
we love one another!

COLOR ME!

SISTERS STICK TOGETHER!

COLOR ME!

I LOVE YOU SIS!

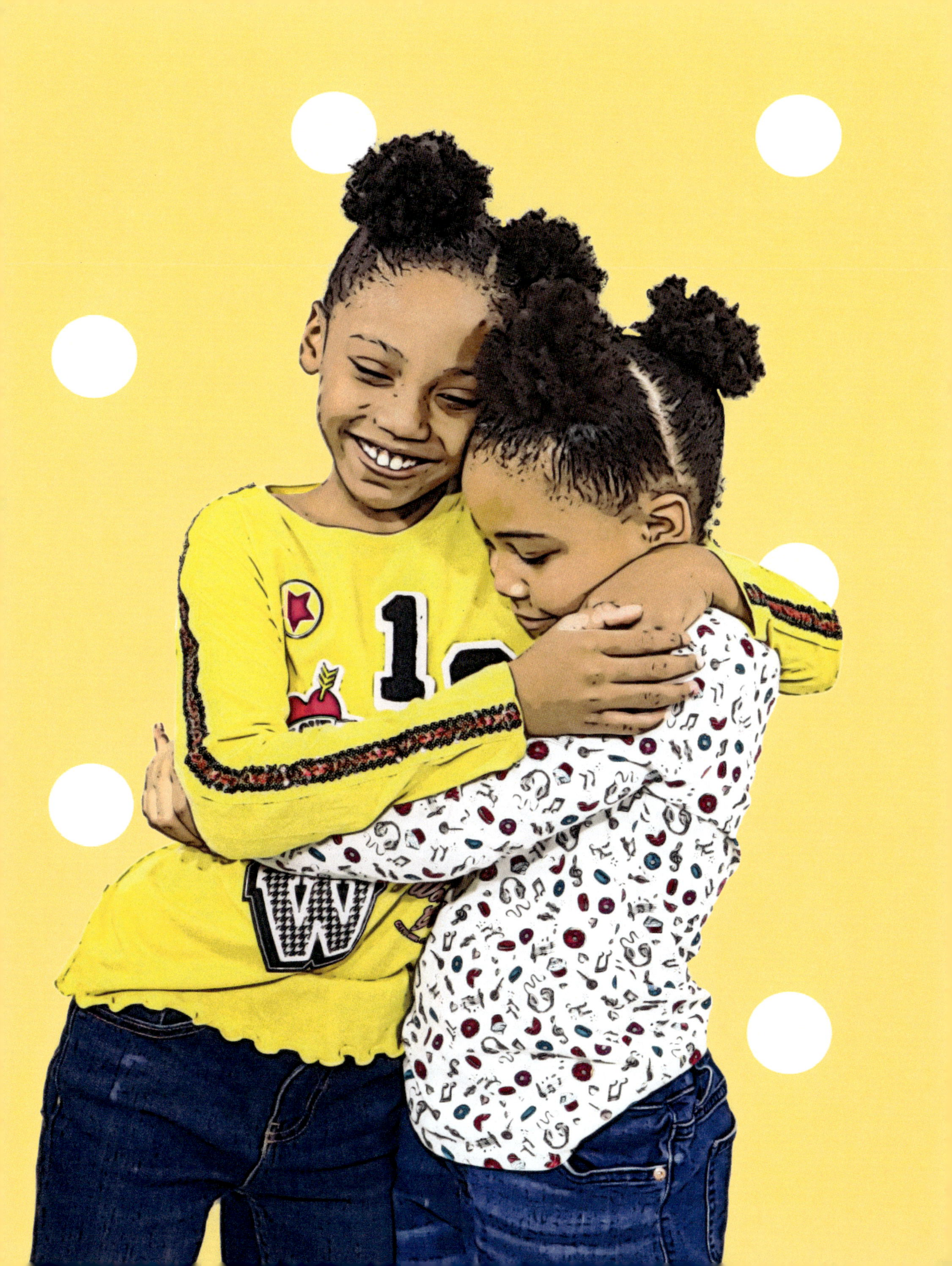

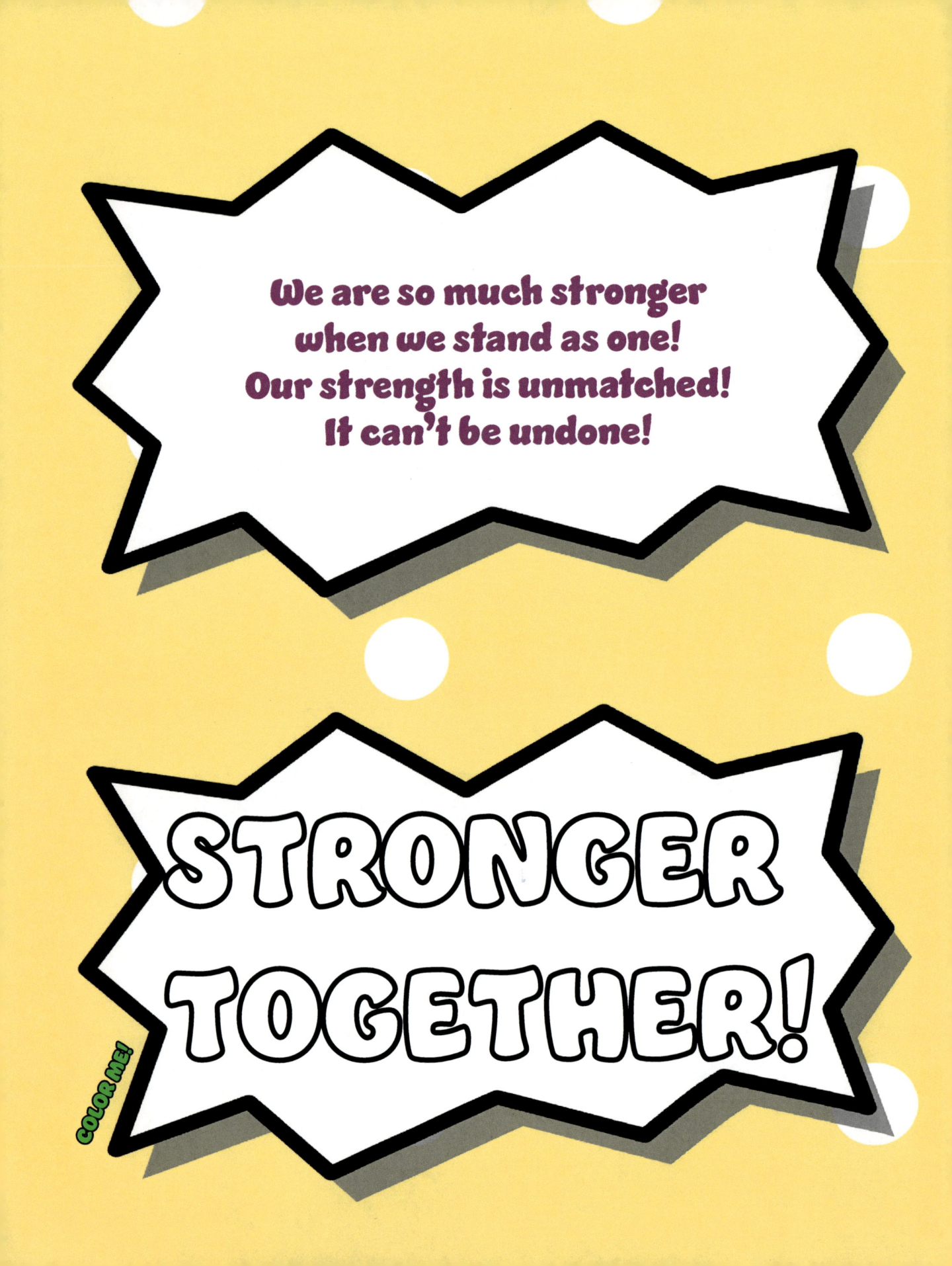

We are so much stronger
when we stand as one!
Our strength is unmatched!
It can't be undone!

STRONGER TOGETHER!

COLOR ME!

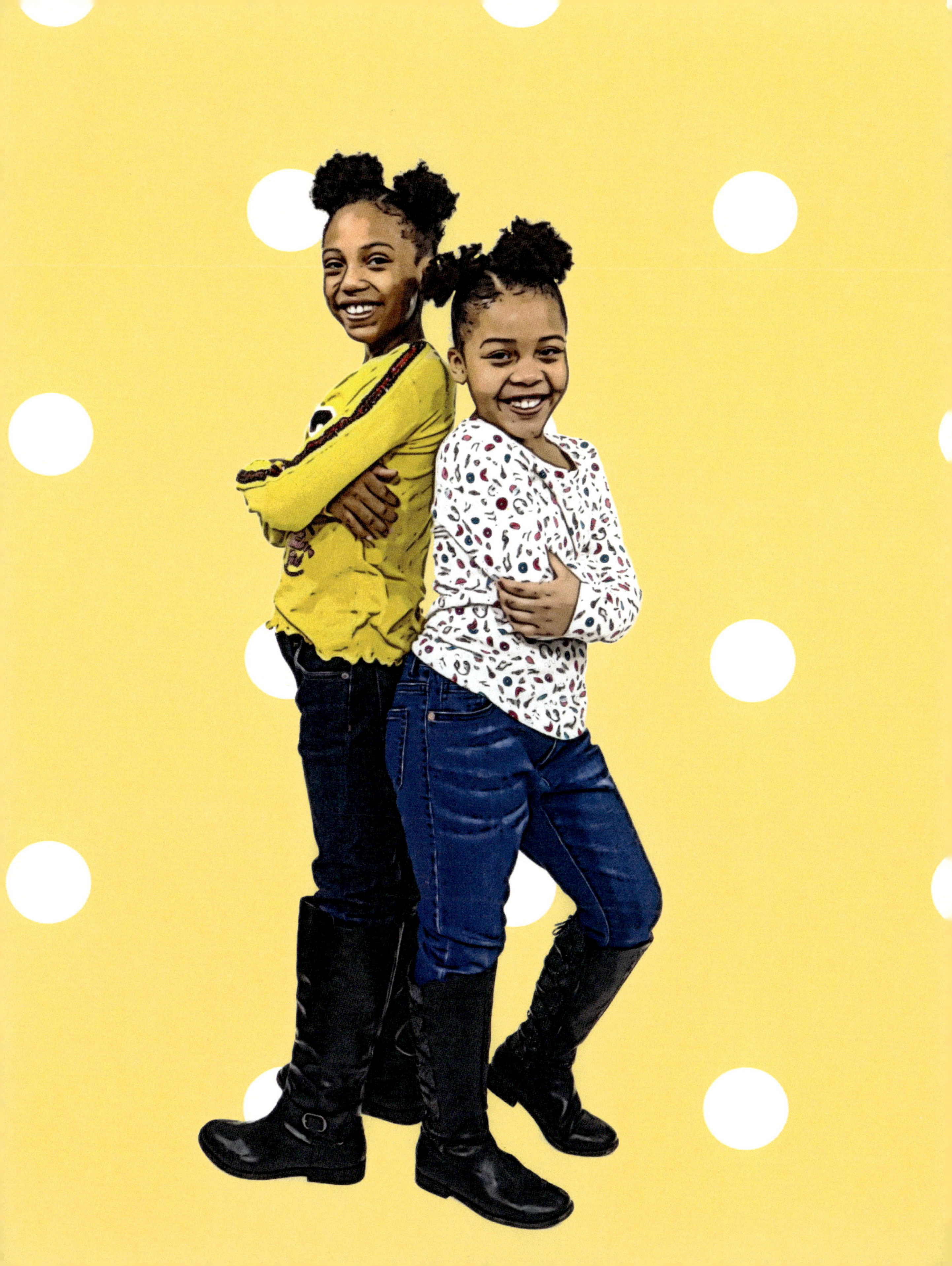

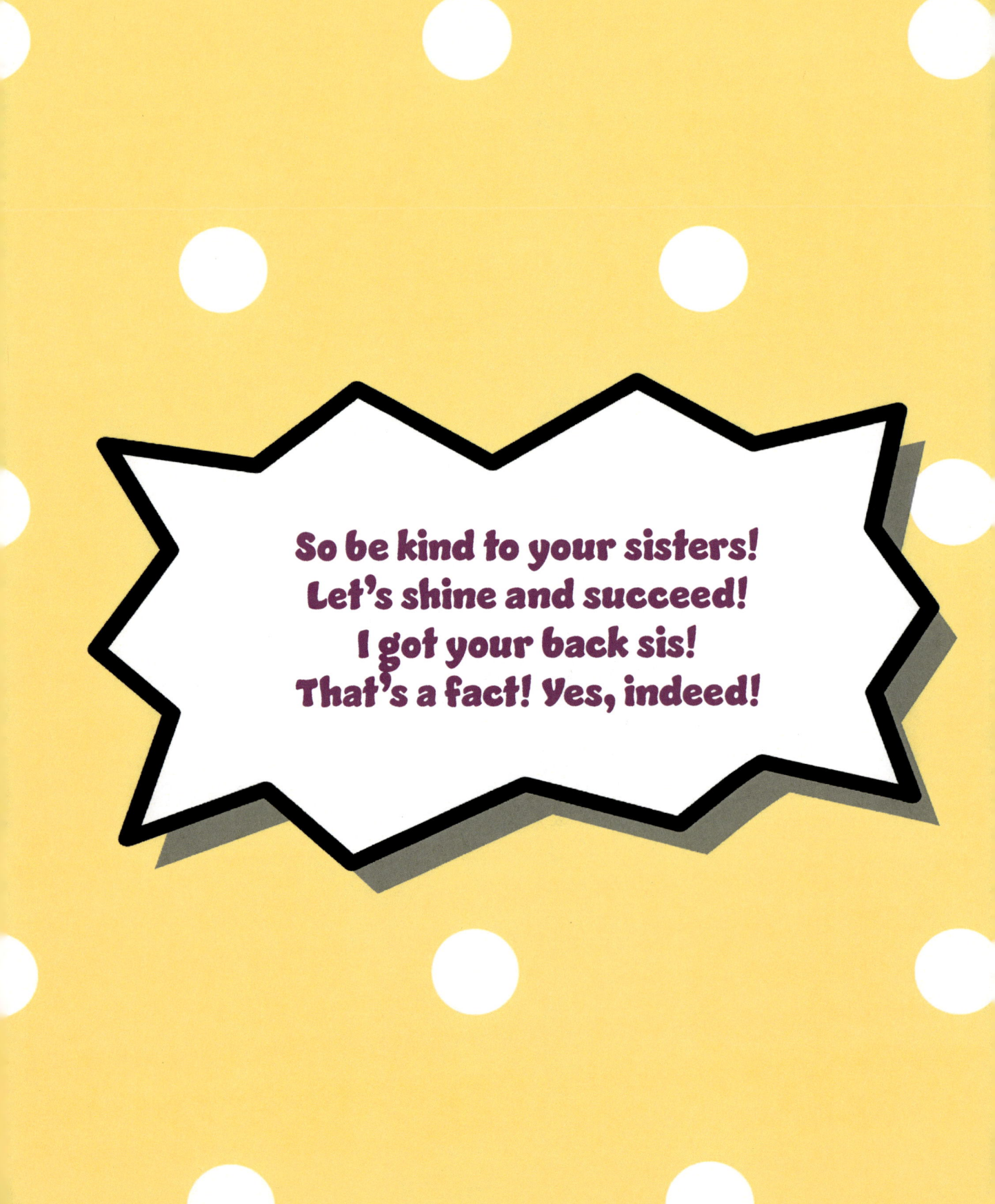

So be kind to your sisters!
Let's shine and succeed!
I got your back sis!
That's a fact! Yes, indeed!

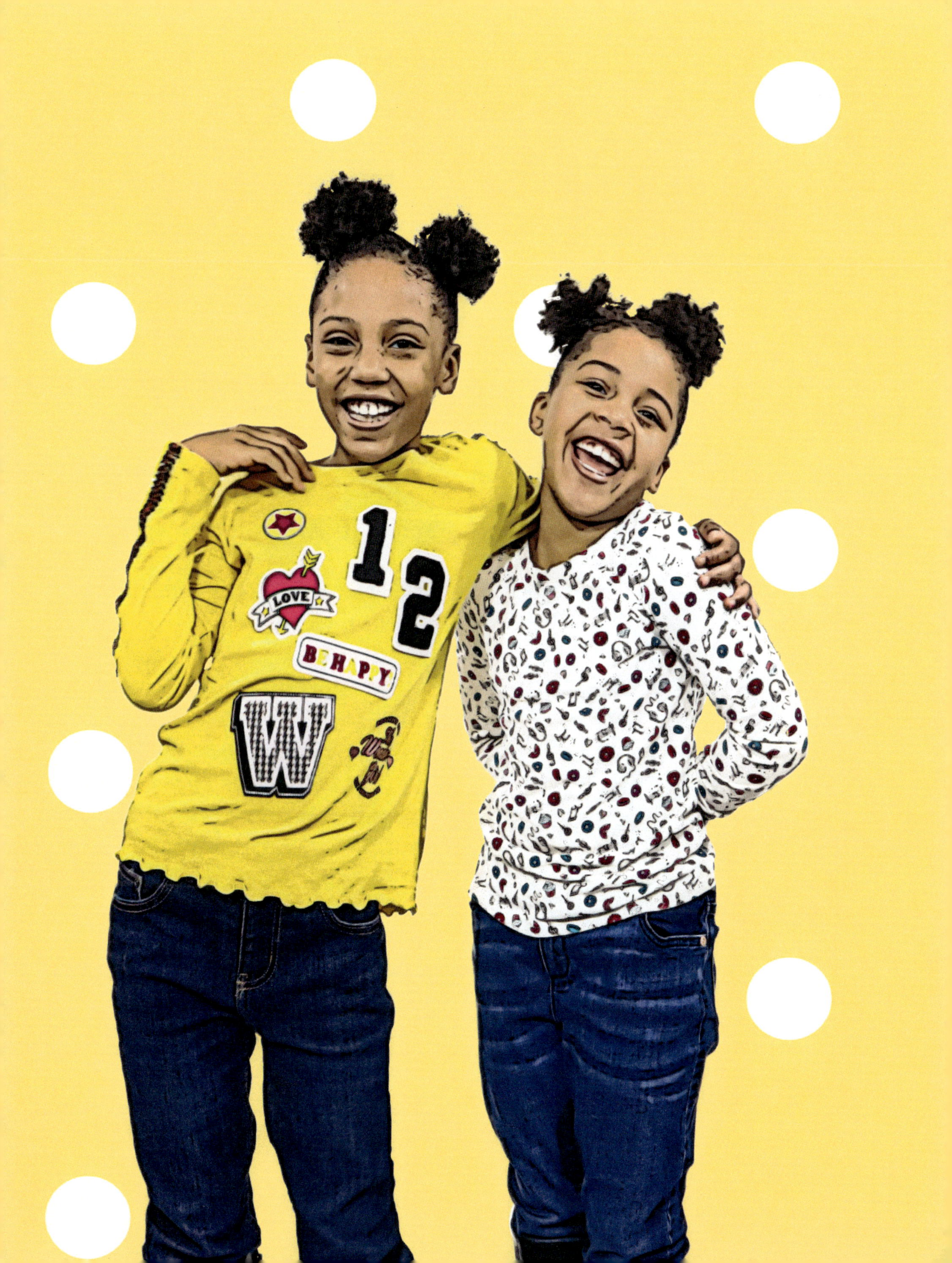
1
2
LOVE
BE HAPPY
W

MEET JAZMINE

Jazmine is a Kansas City, MO native that enjoys telling stories through photography and video!

Most recently, she relocated to Miami, Florida for a short time to pursue her Masters Degree in Communications.

While pursuing her degree, she created a talk show that highlighted the Miami Urban Community.

She also became a mom and decided upon graduation that it was time to come home to Kansas City. Jazmine hopes to continue telling the important stories of her community and beyond.

Website:
jazminec.com

Instagram:
@jazminecproductions

MEET TYIA

Tyia Lashe is a creator from Kansas City, MO. She is a strong believer that words have power and she plans to use hers to change the world.

Tyia's life mission is to empower others to love themselves, believe in themselves, and to know that you can do anything you put your mind to.

Tyia is the creator of the brand, A Beautiful, Wonderful Me, which was created to empower young girls to discover the greatness within themselves.

Instagram: @tyialashe

Website: abwme.com

check out Tyia's other books on Amazon!

SPECIAL THANK YOU TO THIS BOOK'S SPONSORS!

Tiara Weber

Maiya Kelley

Mary Beth Schwartz

Tonya Foster

Lisa Webster

Keila Jackson-Anderson

Furaha Nia

Jerry Avery

Bennie Avery

Made in the USA
Coppell, TX
25 August 2021